Helena Olsen

D0068139

Contents

Introduction

Coziness, connection simplicity, comfort contentment. These are some of the words that you will see as a translation of this rather strange-sounding Danish word. In a way, they are all correct, however the word encompasses so much more than just those ideas or concepts.

In this book, I want to explain to you what hygge is, why it can be life changing in the frantic world we live in today, and the many different ways that you can create hygge in your own life today with little effort.

Hygge – pronounced as "hoo-gah" - is impossible to translate into English in a way that is able to convey all the word means, at least not in a single English word anyway. It is an idea that goes to the very heart of Danish life, a concept that is rooted deep into Danish society.

It is a notion that Danes come to understand from a very early stage of their lives – it is fundamental to who they are, both as individuals and a society. It binds the country together and is one of the reasons why Denmark is consistently declared to be the happiest country on Earth.

Hygge is about removing the source of anything that might cause you to become cross, upset or overwhelmed – to make every effort to create an atmosphere free from stress and one that fosters the more soothing and relaxing things in life.

Hygge is as much a feeling or a state of mind as it is a physical experience. It might be most easily experienced during those cold, long winter months where everyone is making a renewed effort to connect with each other and to bring light and joy into the cold, making every effort to stave off the winter.

It might be a feeling that comes with candlelight and company and food and drink. It might be a walk outside and returning to a hot drink and cake. It might be the effort to appreciate the simpler things in life and being in the moment. Hygge is not about material possessions. It is more of a feeling that is often shared with other people. Although most commonly associated with the winter months, hygge can be experienced anywhere and at any time – an ice-cream on a Summer day, a swim in the ocean, a chat with friends - are all opportunities to enjoy hygge.

Hygge is a way of existing and enjoying life that encompasses many different aspects. Ultimately, it relies on you encouraging an atmosphere where hygge can be created -allowing yourself and others to have every chance of experiencing hygge together. It is seeking out the joy in every situation you find. It is appreciating what you have right now in the present without worry. It is making a conscious effort to escape the relentless and unforgiving pace by which many of us feel overwhelmed.

It is not necessarily about doing things or ticking things off on a list. It is about being in the moment and allowing yourself to take time back. It is about creating a place of warmth, companionship and community, and being able to slow down and relax fully.

This book will offer you thirty-three easy ways to create that feeling of hygge in your own life. It will look at ways inside the house and outside the house. It will consider different ways that you can create hygge within your own life as an individual and also within family and community. It will look at life at home and at work and explain how hygge can be experienced at both.

Read on now for thirty-three ways to create hygge in your life and start living a happier, simpler and more content life today.

Chapter 1 - Internal decoration

Making your home comfy and inviting, doesn't mean that your home won't be stylish. This chapter will consider the various issues to consider when decorating or designing your living spaces and what effect the internal environment of your home can have on you. We will aim for a subtle elegance and style in the room, to which you can then add a little quirkiness and your own personality through accessories or pieces of furniture you might pick up.

#1 Remove clutter

Danish homes tend to opt for a stylish, minimalist look that is tempered by personal touches. You want to avoid living in a totally sterile environment, yet at the same time the last thing you need is to be overwhelmed by objects everywhere that have no place. Ensure that everything in your rooms has a particular home. Make sure the children keep their rooms in order and respect the things they have. Remove things that don't make you happy and replace them with objects that offer a personal connection.

Removing clutter and making order needn't be an exhausting or never-ending process. By bringing in structure and order to the home, you free yourself from the constant burden of looking for places for things to go and moving them from one place to another. You don't have to be continually cleaning or worrying about the state of your home. The clutter that surrounds you starts to weigh you down – removing it can be liberating and creates a feeling of freedom and release.

Consider a "less is more" philosophy. Having tens of cushions on your seating arrangements is unlikely to be effective. Remove those cushions that you no longer particularly like or those that are no longer at their best. Reduce the number to three or four that really evoke strong emotions in you, that are a pleasure to feel or look at. Remove the others to storage if you are sure you still like them, otherwise get rid of them.

You only want items in your rooms that are going to make you feel positive and add to your general well-being. Worrying about where things go, being annoyed that others are not helping you keep everything tidy or with yourself that your own living space is not right, will only make you feel stressed – this is exactly what we are trying to avoid over the long winter months.

Thinking carefully about how to maximize the amount of natural light in your house is important. Daylight is a precious commodity over winter and the more you can get into your house, the better you will feel. Don't obstruct the light that is coming in with large objects on your window sills. Consider removing heavy curtains or blinds entirely. Opt for a much lighter replacement cotton curtains in white or plain colors that will allow the light to bounce off them into the room. You might think about shutters as insulation for night time.

The desire to enhance light is also shown in the choice of colors for the walls in the home. In Danish homes, these are often white that will reflect whatever natural light comes into the room during the shorter days. If you have color on the walls, it is often a rather muted hue. Pale blue or grey on the walls are also common and work to complement the calm atmosphere created throughout the home.

If you are looking to add just a little dash of really bright color, consider using an accessory such as a cushion or two. Black and white is common combination with which you could experiment. A black and white rug will look stunning when placed within the muted environment. A beautiful vase of fresh flowers will also add color and vitality to the room.

Try different forms and sizes of lamps. Lamps are so useful because they can be moved around and positioned as you see fit with the minimum of fuss. You could configure certain places in the room to facilitate reading for example, with a table light and a comfy chair. By using light effectively, you can easily transform a room from daytime to night time. A lamp also allows you to bring the eye to certain aspects of the room you might want to emphasize. This accent lighting can be very effective at highlighting a particular picture or a fireplace.

You could investigate fitting dimmer switches on your lights to change the intensity of the lighting easily and effectively. If you wanted to go really high-tech there are lights on the market that can change color according to the time of the day or what mood you might like to project. There are also timers for lights that can be controlled remotely. When these lights work together, you can create a variety of ambiences with the minimum of effort.

Avoid the harsh, strip lights that cast a sterile white glare everywhere – they will do nothing to enhance anyone's mood. Low hung lights from the ceiling that cast a warm glow over the table are far more effective and avoid making the kitchen feel like a hospital.

However, you don't have to go ripping out all your lights because they don't quite create the right mood. A very simple step is to consider the warmth of your bulbs. All lights can be placed on the Kelvin Scale where the lower the number, the warmer the light is and the higher the number, the purer the white becomes.

If you want to create a cozy atmosphere in any room, simply swapping the bulbs out to something around the 2700 Kelvin mark will create a yellower and warmer light straightaway with the minimum of effort.

The use of candles in the home is one of the most recognisable features of hygge. The Danes use candles the whole year round and everywhere you go, you will see candles rather than the harsh light that can come from overhead lighting. Candles allow you to create a source of light wherever you wish and can be used to bring focus to certain parts of the room while concealing others.

Candles will instantly add a feeling of inviting warmth and calmness into a room. They can reduce stress and their flickering light produces an intimacy which cannot be replicated elsewhere. In addition to the warming light they cast, candles can also be scented.

Experiment with a few to find ones you like – I enjoy vanilla-scented candles – but try to avoid candles that are artificially scented. Choose candles that are created with natural essential oils such as lavender, rose, ylang ylang, bergamot, or chamomile.

If possible, opt for a soy based candle or beeswax candle, rather than paraffin candles that can release soot particles along with acetone, benzene and toluene. Soy candles are made from vegetable oil, not petroleum oil, and don't need any chemicals for their scent.

You will also find they burn far more slowly and cleanly than paraffin, giving you better value for money.

Candles come in a variety of colors which can also be used to alter mood. A white or light pastel colored candle is a calming sight that works with the scent and light to strengthen the feeling of warmth and comfort.

Candles do bring in an element of danger with their naked flames which can put off many families with young children or pets. Artificial candles will help you solve this problem. They are not quite the same as the real thing of course, but they present no fire-risk and can also be placed in locations where it would be too dangerous to place real candles. They are battery driven and can be used with timers so the room is beautifully lit and ready for you when you return home from work or a trip out.

There are different types of candles and it can be highly effective to use these varieties in various locations in the room. You could have a large pillar candle or a combination of candles placed together in the corner of a kitchen for example, to create intimacy at the table. Votive candles are smaller than pillars and are placed in glass containers to burn. They will burn for around 10 -15 hours.

Tea light candles look lovely and can be dotted all over the room in attractive candle holders. You will see these everywhere in Denmark and they can make any room beautiful in comparison to the cold and dark outside. An array of tea lights or even just a couple in a room can have a wonderfully pleasing and calming effect.

Experiment until you find the places that look best in your rooms and you will find people drawn there for conversation or simply just for quiet reflection as they bask in the candles' flickering light.

#4 Flooring

Heavy, dark carpet will act as a black hole for light. Traditionally, Danish homes are associated with wood which adds a warmth to the room that is hard to reproduce by other means. Consider removing carpet and opting for floor boards instead. You can either sand these down and polish them up to reflect even more light, or perhaps paint them white. If you have the choice, a lighter wood is ideal both for extra light reflection and being better at concealing scratches and the odd bump.

Wood is a great insulator, so having it as your floor will increase the general warmth of the room as opposed to using tiles. There are many green alternatives that can be used for flooring as well, such as bamboo or cork. You can install underfloor heating although be careful when you make your choice. Certain types of soft wood are best avoided, as they could change in size with the heat.

Another very popular choice at the moment is a concrete floor which is low maintenance and long-lasting. It can be polished as well to reflect the light beautifully and is perfect for radiating heat. It may conjure up images of being cold and unwelcoming, however it can have virtually any finish applied and it is also very economical to install.

Whichever type of flooring you have or are thinking of installing, be sure to complement it with a warming and textured rug, that will also be a piece of art in its own right. A large rug can become a focal point, that invites people in to congregate around a seating area. Make sure it goes well with your furniture and color schemes. Try to ensure it is big enough that at least that the front legs of all the furniture can fit on the rug and that your guests' resting feet will be able to enjoy the warmth it brings.

#5 Mirrors

Mirrors work wonders in appearing to increase the light and space in any room. Placing a large mirror next to a window can create the illusion of a second window. The same effect can be had by placing the mirror opposite a window. The sunlight will be reflected straight back into the room, increasing the light and warmth. Using mirrors of the same size placed opposite each other is extremely effective in increasing light and depth as the reflections go on as far as the eye can see.

Experiment with placement of your mirrors. This will vary from room to room, but allowing the mirror to reflect firelight can be particularly effective at increasing the perception of space and warmth. If mirrors are placed close by to a light source, it will reflect it off at an angle, amplifying the light. When used together with candles, mirrors can look quite beautiful.

You don't need to limit yourself to just mirrors. Any item that is reflective will have the same effect. Photograph frames, picture frames, candle holders – the shinier they are, the more light they will generate for you. Do ensure you keep the mirrors and windows as clean as possible to prevent any dirt filtering out the light you are working hard to bring into the room.

The use of texture in a room can be very effective. Try small items like a fluffy rug for example, or perhaps adding shells or branches to a table as decoration. You can use cushions or throws made from different substances to add a hint of bold color and a different feel to the room.

Cushions are ideal because they are inexpensive and they are available in such a wide variety of colors and materials. You could try three or four different cushions and see how they work together or swap and mix as you see fit. The key point is not to go overboard. Throwing twenty cushions on the seating arrangements will do nothing but create mess and feeling of disorder.

Adding frames or clocks or photo frames to the walls will have a similar effect. If they are made of wood it will add to the general coziness of the room, as will any natural substance. You will no doubt be using plants and candles already, which will also add a different texture of their own to the room and a uniqueness to your space.

Aim for a subtle approach but one that has an impact on your guests as they walk in. Less is generally more in this case. If you find the room a little overwhelming, remove items one by one and ensure you stick to the natural substances such as wood or natural fibers in your rugs and cushions.

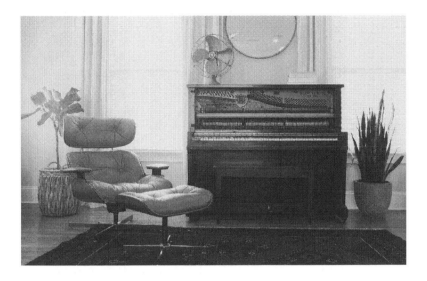

The Danish are renowned for their furniture design. Names such as Arne Jacobsen and Hans Wegner are revered for their designs today still and although the furniture is far from cheap, it is possible to pick up more reasonably priced reproductions. Consider how you are going to spend your budget. You might prefer to splash out on a couple of quality pieces or spread the budget around a little more evenly. Always buy objects that are going to make you happy when you use or look at them.

Danish furniture is famous for its clean lines, simple design and comfort. It has a timeless look that still feels modern today and fits beautifully into today's homes. It is lightweight and can be moved around easily. The combination of simplicity, comfort and style is perfect for the home and its presence will always give you something beautiful to look at.

#8 How to choose the right scents

Scent can be very powerful and provocative. Scents evoke memories and can lend that extra feeling of warmth, comfort and security to a home. The right scent will help you relax and create a warming atmosphere in any part of your house. In addition to creating scents through candles, you could use your favorite essential oils in a warm bath or any location through the use of a strategically placed reed diffuser.

It could be the smell of lavender or eucalyptus or a blended oil that you prefer. If you fancy a particularly Christmas-like scent, you could opt for frankincense or myrrh There are so many different varieties that will appeal to each person on an individual basis. Try a number out and gauge opinion on what works best in your own home.

Having a touch of nature in your home can be most beneficial. Using plants inside can improve air quality, reconnect you to nature and create a general air of vitality which can be invaluable in the winter months.

There are numerous studies which show that indoor plants can have many beneficial health effects. They help with breathing, aid focus and concentration and can prevent common ailments like a cold.

NASA's own Clear Air study revealed that plants remove trichloroethylene, benzene, formaldehyde, xylene and ammonia from the air, all of which are connected with complaints such as headaches. The peace lily, English lily, bamboo palm, gerbera daisy, chrysanthemum or spider plant can be particularly effective.

Flowers on the table are a wonderful talking point and beautiful decoration. They look stunning when arranged in a glass vase and will offer cheer and happiness to anyone who sees them. Consider taking a small bunch to work if possible, to remind yourself of home and to make the office a little less sterile and a little more welcoming

.

Chapter 2 – Hygge Food and Drink

Food and drink is an essential component of hygge- not just the consumption of it, but also the thought that goes into a welcoming meal for guests or family. Use the preparation of your meal as an opportunity to get your guests involved in the whole process.

Don't worry about the kitchen being messy when the doorbell rings – getting people into the kitchen, gaining their input and talking together only adds to that feeling of warmth and togetherness. In many ways, it's not so much about what you are actually cooking, and more about the process of creating a meal together.

Baking itself is a therapeutic act which requires concentration and effort. It doesn't allow for negative thoughts and making a nourishing meal together is normally a very positive experience for all involved. In addition to the mental benefits, you know exactly what's in your food, it's healthier than shop-bought products and free from artificial preservatives.

#10 Home baking

Cooking a meal from scratch is a highly rewarding process and when friends and family join in, it is an experience that is enjoyed together by all. People come together not just over the eating of the food, but its preparation. Enjoy the fact that certain meals can take a long time to prepare.

We all think of the tremendously inviting smell of baked bread or a cake as we enter a house, but don't limit your cooking just to those type of foods. Consider the foods that are in season and can be found naturally around you. Use local produce where you can and you will be able to create something nourishing and delicious.

Consider using those vegetables which are in season over the winter months. These include buttercup squash, Brussels sprouts, collard green, kale, leeks, sweet potato, turnips and winter squash.

Foods such as cabbage with its high quantities of vitamin C and K and folate are still widely available in the winter months and taste great when added to a salad or a stir fry. These vegetables are packed with healthy nutrients and with a little care and attention can be made into highly popular dishes, either as an accompaniment or just by themselves. They are also relatively cheap to buy and they store well.

Rather than buy pre-packaged meat, talk to the butcher about the origins of the meat on sale and how it might best be used. You can find the perfect cut of cheaper meat that will be delicious after a longer period of cooking. Nothing is quite so comfy as a naturally made stew or soup with warm bread after you have been for a bracing walk in the cold.

When it comes to cakes and desserts, life in Denmark is one of abundance. From their famous, wonderfully fragrant cinnamon rolls to chocolate cake to pastries of course, there is a true celebration of food and a recognition of the joy a lovingly cooked meal can bring to all at the table.

#11 Making time to cook

There are few times in the year when you get a genuine chance to make a meal that takes a reasonable amount of time, however the winter months and the vacation period can offer just that opportunity. If you get the time, you could even make bigger quantities and freeze for later in the year when you are a little more rushed, but could still use a hearty meal to keep you going.

I am a big fan of cookbooks – I have lots at home and enjoy flicking through them and admiring the pictures, even if I recognize I'm unlikely to find the chance to get to cook them in the near future. I do make a note of them however, and resolve to return to them when I have a little more time with family and friends.

I write the references down in a notebook near the bookshelf so I'm able to go back when I know I can give the necessary effort for the recipes to be a success.

#12 The perfect hot drink

The necessary complement to a perfect meal is of course the right drink. The very essence of hygge might be represented by the clutching of a steaming cup of coffee as you gaze out of a candlelit room into the forbidding dark that lies outside. Coffee and cake are absolute staples of Danish life and enjoying these little treats with others strengthens the idea of companionship and comfort.

Don't treat a coffee break as a meaningless interval between whatever else you happened to be doing at the time, but make it a deliberate moment in your day. Consider inviting people over to enjoy the experience with you. Even a relative stranger could be welcomed for a morning or afternoon coffee.

When making your tea or coffee, it is customary to make an effort to enjoy the moment, either alone or with friends. If you are going to prepare tea, don't just stick a teabag in a cup and pour the water over – go to the bother of making tea properly with a teapot. The tea will taste better, it's much more attractive to look at a teapot, and you can have a second cup as well which has remained warm the whole time.

Try out various varieties of tea – there are different types of herbal teas as well as a decaffeinated version for late at night if you prefer. The range of teas include white, green, black chamomile, oolong or Echinacea to name just a few. Even tea just bought in teabag form can taste quite different across the various brands so experiment until you find one that suits. Tea will even taste slightly differently depending on what type of cup or mug you use.

The process of tea is a ritual that is designed to make the tasting of tea the best it can possibly be, while at the same time allowing time and opportunity for friendships to be formed. It appeals to sight, smell and taste and will enhance your enjoyment of tea greatly. Here are a few tips I have picked up over the years for tea making.

Use fresh water directly from the tap or better still filtered water. Don't use water that has previously been boiled.

Don't let the water over-boil in the kettle. Try and stop it just before it stops boiling. If it does boil, then give it just a minute to cool down slightly before pouring it over your tea leaves or tea bag.

Add the water to the teapot first and the cups you will be using to warm them up. Pour away the remaining water.

Add in the tea to the teapot and pour the hot water over the top. Allow to steep in the pot for the recommended time (this will vary from tea to tea), but about five minutes will be fine.

If you are going to have milk, then put the milk in first. Be careful not to overwhelm the taste of the delicate tea.

If you are using leaf tea, then strain the tea into the cups and serve to your guests.

Of course, many people prefer coffee although there have been entire books written on how to make coffee as well as some very expensive kitchen gadgets that claim to make the perfect cup. Everyone has their own opinion on what makes the ultimate cup of coffee and what method you use. The important thing is the time and effort that you put in to show that meeting with people means something. Indicating that you are going to an extra effort for the preparation of something so simple as a hot drink is important. It's a clear signal that people matter to you and that you are willing to give up time, that most precious commodity of all, to be with them.

#13 Drinking Glogg

The Danes are big beer drinkers. The most famous brand is probably Carlsberg, however the darker beers are also becoming popular along with various local microbreweries which produce all kinds of beer, some of which can be very strong. However, over the winter months one of the most popular Danish hot drinks is Glogg. This wonderfully warming mulled wine is very easy and cheap to make and will go a long way to ward off the cold nights. You can have this simmering away on the stove as guests arrive and it will prove an immediate success.

There isn't one particular recipe for Glogg, but at its heart is red wine with various spices including cinnamon, cardamom, cloves, raisins and almonds. You can also add port and brandy if you wish. Simmer the lot together for a couple of hours and serve as people arrive. You can replenish the vat as it goes down as the spices last a long time. Don't worry about using an expensive red wine. A cheap one will taste just as good once it has combined with the various spices and other alcohol that you add to it.

Chapter 3 —Hygge Activities Inside the Home

Taking the time to connect and be with people is vital to recreate the feeling of hygge within the home. This chapter contains a number of activities which will be enjoyable for the whole family.

#14 Lose electronic gadgets

Aim to restrict their usage. This is a simple step to say, but perhaps less easy to put into practice. Nonetheless, it's difficult to promote relationships between family and friends if everyone is staring at a 4-inch screen for 8 hours a day. Of course, there can be a time and a place for a cell phone or iPod or tablet, but as a general rule these should be out of mind, out of sight.

If this starts a dispute with the kids, then you could offer their devices back as a very short incentive, after some family time together or once you have returned from a long walk. Place a time limit on them however, and ensure that nobody disappears for the evening in isolation. Nobody can properly connect with the present if they are focused on a screen and worried about missing something "important" on some distant social network.

Allow everyone to get away from their electronic gadgets for a time, reconnect with each other and appreciate what is really important. It's surprising how quickly people adapt to putting them down and feeling freed from the constant beeping and interruptions that distract and demand attention.

#15 Play games as a family

Hygge is all about togetherness and a sense of community. Engage in activities that require group participation. Get the entire family involved in a traditional game that requires teamwork and thoughts. Look for old favorites that need interaction to be a success. Ensure everyone can play from all ages.

A pack of cards can prove tremendously popular and will give you access to games as simple as Snap up to the complexities of Bridge. The idea is to get everyone playing and prevent little pockets of isolation as everyone disappears on their own to watch television or play computer games.

There are also plenty of games that don't require any equipment at all, so no need to worry about storage or who is going to do the packing up. Games such as Charades can be played by all ages and are the very definition of group participation, as everyone shouts out an answer and then has a go.

Word games where you make up stories following a particular pattern are good fun and great for developing linguistic skills. For example, you could create a story where each person must say the next word as long as its first letter follows the order of the alphabet e.g. A Bear Came Down Eagerly Finding Great Humans Inside. The next word would have to begin with the letter "J".

Memory games such as "I went to the shops" work really well in groups Each person starts by listing everything that has been previously bought by everyone else at this imaginary shop and then adds one more thing that they bought themselves. The list gradually gets longer and longer until people end up being knocked out when they can't remember the whole list.

Wink Murder is also a lot of fun. One person is secretly selected to be the murderer. Have everyone close their eyes at the beginning and you can tap that person on the shoulder so they know they are the one. The murderer can kill people by winking at them. Once killed, you must count to 5 and then pretend to be dead. The aim of the game is for the other players to work out who the killer is before they suffer the same fate. They are not allowed to talk to each other or team up nor wink at other players.

You probably have particular family favorites of your own that may not get played very much during other busy periods of the year. Use the time you have together to bring these games back to promote a feeling of fun and togetherness.

#16 Being creative

If you have the chance, then being creative with arts and crafts can be a lot of fun on a cold and wet afternoon for both kids and adults. It will allow everyone to use their imagination to create whatever takes their fancy. Everyone can work together and communicate in order to fulfil a particular task. In addition, it is a great learning tool with opportunities to discuss mathematical concepts or enhance language skills, as well as a bringing a wonderful sense of achievement and success when the masterpiece is finally complete.

Allow everyone to use whatever materials or implements you have to hand. These are readily obtainable from shops, but some essentials might include paint, crayons, pencils, different colored paper, safety scissors, glue along with perhaps some beads, string, thread, toothpicks or aluminium foil. Have a good look around the house to see what you have lying around – I've had great results before, by turning to the food cupboards and using little pasta shapes when supplies are running low.

Creating art, of any form, is a great way to relax and relieve stress. It enables you to focus on one thing which prevents you worrying about other issues in life. The recent trend in adult coloring books is just one example of where people are seeking calming activities to gain some respite from the stresses of modern life.

Art can be created on your own of course, but there is added pleasure in spending time together and creating art as a group. Being creative, boosting self-esteem and being together is very hyggelig. It is something everyone, of any age, will find mentally stimulating and challenging, as well as a lot of fun.

#17 Reading for joy

There might be little more that can successfully bring hygge into your life than reading a book. The pleasure it can bring is enhanced when you are comfortably snug and warm, accompanied by your favorite drink, in a muted room lit by candlelight.

Reading a book takes you away from the present and into a different reality where anything is possible and the worries of the future can be put aside. Reading is an indulgence that can truly be savored. Allowing yourself the luxury of that time will only serve to increase your own mental well-being.

Another excellent reading activity that works particularly well with children, but can be used with anyone at all, is reading aloud. Everyone likes stories read to them, no matter what age, and I have always found this a wonderful activity at bringing people together and sparking conversations.

Such talks often lead to places you may not have expected and allow people to share their personal opinions and thoughts, within the structured context of a book discussion.

Gather people around a table or somewhere comfortable where everyone can see you. You might like to spend a minute talking about the author, perhaps just reading from the back cover will be enough, to spark interest in your audience.

Then read for around ten to fifteen minutes or longer if everyone seems to be maintaining their interest. At this point, I will often stop, put the book down for a minute and just ask a couple of questions to gauge opinion and interest in proceedings.

Check your audience understands exactly what is happening or if there are any particularly complex words you have to explain. Failure to follow the plot will result in your listeners losing focus rapidly. At that point you can stop or continue as you see fit. I often take a break, then resume later on, when you have receptive and focused listeners.

Of course, you will want to pitch the right book to the right audience. There is no point going too highbrow for very young children or the opposite for adults. Ask questions beforehand to see what type of books people are interested in and think of the different ages to which you will be reading.

Particular favorites of mine have been young adult books or even mildly scary ghost stories which seem to appeal to both young and old. The Harry Potter series for example, has been a regular read over the past few years and has an appeal that seems to transcend age.

Feel free to throw open the floor to anyone else who would like to have a go. They don't have to read an entire book. Perhaps a favorite chapter might be enough. I normally find younger children are very keen to have a go reading to an audience and relish the fact they have a captive audience.

I also like to keep a reading record, somewhere quite visible, of all the books we have read together. This gives your listeners a sense of achievement and progress, and will inspire them to hear more and participate. Listing the books to come can be another method to give them something to look forward to. Choosing series of books can be very effective. Once your listeners get to know the characters and hear the plot progressing from chapter to chapter, book to book, they will be very keen to know how it all finishes.

#18 Have an indoor picnic

My family adores picnics. We love the entire process. Making the food, packing it all up, safe in the knowledge that it will soon be consumed in the open air, heading out for a walk or bike ride and then sitting down together and eating our way through lunch. Picnics are always good outside, but if the weather is truly inhospitable, then it can be great fun to have an indoor picnic.

Get the kids to contribute their homemade efforts to the picnic basket, spread out a rug and the food on the floor. Include things you might not expect to find normally at a picnic. Try bringing along sushi, or beautifully cut sandwiches, sliced fruit, seeds and raisins, cheeses and of course chocolate. Lots of chocolate is always a winner.

Having an indoor picnic is great for a change and will spark conversations between family and friends – especially once you retire to the kitchen for a glass of wine.

In today's world of hastily written emails that are typed in thirty seconds and read even more quickly, it can be a delight to receive a letter through the post that has been hand-written. The writing of letters can be pleasurable as well. Take the time out to plan a little what you are writing, to construct your thoughts and ensure you are delivering the message you are looking to convey. Take that little extra time to enjoy the moments it takes to write something that genuinely means something.

Of course, not all letters have to be epic pieces of writing. If that feels a little overwhelming, then start off with smaller projects. Use old postcards you have lying around and send a quick card to friends and family. I always put any I receive on display as a reminder of distant places and people. Emails tend to head straight for a folder on my hard drive, never to be seen again, or worse still, disappear with a casual press of the delete button.

Kids love to send letters and their adult recipients enjoy receiving them even more. Sit them down and have them send a little thank you letter for a birthday or Christmas present. Even a quick "hello – it's me!" indicates the time taken to construct a letter, put a stamp on it and walk out in the cold to place it in the post-box. My kids always enjoyed cutting up Christmas cards and using the pictures as postcards to send off as a thank you to their various benefactors. Let them decorate them as they see fit, then take a stroll to the post box to send them off.

#20 Hygge music

Music is extremely powerful. It can evoke all sorts of varied emotions and thoughts in people, as well as memories of a particular place or time. It is something we are all naturally drawn to and each of us enjoys our own particular type of music or singer.

This might be a good time to dig out that old record player you or someone you know may have lying around and spin the vinyl for that true analogue warmth and crackle you can only get from playing records.

Of course, you can just use modern technology if you've no access to anything else, but there is something special about taking the time to flick through those big album covers, choose the record and then take the time to get the record player working.

My all-time favorite hygge song is "This Must Be The Place" by the fabulous Talking Heads. Something about the way the song is written, the music, the lyrics and the personal memories it holds for me, makes me feel happy and contented every single time.

Constructing your own list of similar songs is a great activity to carry out with friends who will no doubt introduce you to their own favorite songs.

If you can play your own music, then all the better! Simply jamming along in a group, playing the piano or just singing a song together can be a great way to make connections in a group of people and can be enjoyed by young or old alike.

#21 Watching TV

There might be times when the call of television is too much to resist and you find yourself bowing to pressure to allow some time to watch the screen. There is no need to be overly obsessive with preventing people watching television of course, but if you are going to watch, then ensure they are programs that will be enjoyed by everyone present.

TV shows that involve competition and a degree of audience participation might be ideal. Programs where you can share and exchange opinions about the competitors would be great for example. Use the television to foster discussion and talk between yourselves.

If it's just you, curling up under a blanket with a hot drink and chocolate while you binge on the latest Netflix show can be extremely hyggelig in itself. Grab your favorite feel-good film and put it on the big screen to enjoy.

Chapter 4 – Hygge Outside

Just because it's winter, doesn't mean that you can't exercise and get the blood pumping round your body. That feeling of warmth and coziness will only be enhanced when you come in from the cold glowing with the effort of exercise. This chapter contains suggestions for activities outside the house that will be enjoyable for all.

#22 Be active

Take a walk in the park and connect with the natural world around you. Leave any electronic devices you may have at home. Allow yourself just to be outdoors and enjoy the natural world around you.

You can walk by yourself of course or take friends and family with you. Make it a communal activity which will encourage participation and conversation. You could knock on a neighbour's door and see if they would like to accompany you to encourage that idea of community and togetherness.

Take the opportunity to grab any hint of sunlight you can get during the winter months. However, even if you can't organise it during the day with people, it can be great to go out at night and see the lights and walk in the darkness too. Just ensure the hot drinks and blankets are there waiting for you upon your return.

#23 Choosing the right clothing

Hygge clothing is all about comfort. The choices are immense, but wearing something that is warming, soft and luxurious is going to make going outside in the cold much, more appealing. Don't obsess about latest fashions or what you think you should be wearing for a particular occasion. If you are going out in the wet, try to have warm clothing that you can put on immediately as you return.

If you fancy going Danish-style for a while, try wearing a black skirt or trousers with a chunky sweater and a thick scarf. Ensure your gloves are fleece-lined and offer genuine protection against the cold. Silk underwear is truly amazing. Incredibly comfortable and warm, it will offer great insulation against your skin. Add your thicker layers on top, finishing with the sweater. Make sure your footwear is appropriate. If you're in a cold climate, a decent pair of

44

boots is essential to ward off the cold and offer substantial grip against the snow and ice. Nothing will destroy hygge more than slipping over when walking on ice and hurting yourself.

If you take a stroll in the cold and the wet, remember the Scandinavian expression – "there's no such thing as bad weather, only bad clothes". Get yourself rugged up with the scarf, hat, gloves, woolly socks. Taking exercise even when the weather isn't great is an essential part of hygge and makes coming home to a warm and inviting house all the more satisfying.

#24 Take day trips

As pleasing as it is to hibernate a little over the winter period, people still like to get out and about with a few day trips. Plan these carefully and ensure they are appropriate for the entire family as the last thing you want is a bored teenager complaining about the latest exhibition to which he or she is being dragged.

Consult first and if you can't agree, then try and fit in a couple of items during the one day. You could go to a museum for example, and then go to the movies to try and keep everyone happy. If you are heading off into the countryside, just ensure you have all your necessary supplies and provisions! A day trip is a great opportunity for families to re-connect and do something fun as a group.

The arrival of the cold, ice and snow gives you a chance to get engaged in all sorts of winter sports that weren't previously possible. Try ice skating or even skiing. Arrange to meet people for an afternoon together. Take the kids outside and build a snowman or simply have a snowball fight in the cold. Take the sled out and seek out a hill to conquer. View the arrival of the cold as an additional chance to meet and exercise together.

There can be few modes of transport that are more hyggelig than the bicycle. A bike allows you to be at one with nature and breathe in the air as you travel without being cooped up in a car. It's a fun form of exercise that gets the blood pumping and can clear your head as you travel. Cycling can be done as a family with joint rides on an afternoon out to the park. If you feel like you're not quite up to cycling long distances, you can even add a motor to your bike to assist you as you go up hills.

Riding a bike in in the sunlight with your heart pumping as you get your exercise, no matter what season, is a truly wonderful experience. It may have been a while since you last cycled, but try it again and you will enjoy the ride. There are always plenty of cycling groups around, with people who are prepared to give generously of their time and expertise. Cycling in a group adds to a sense of community and togetherness and is highly rewarding.

Chapter 5 – Hygge through Conversation

One of the many concepts of hygge is thinking of others and fostering a community, not only within your own home, but also in the local neighborhood. If you are alone, then the winter and the festive season can be a difficult time, both physically with the cold and mentally with the isolation that it can bring. This is only re-inforced by others appearing to have an especially great time. This chapter focuses on making links with others and the vital importance of good conversation and communication.

#26 Hygge in the neighborhood

Forging links of some description with your neighbours or those close to you will be beneficial both to you and them. It doesn't mean popping round there for hours and hours or cooking every meal for them, but just sitting down and have a slow cup of coffee and a chat can do wonders to ward off loneliness and depressing thoughts at that time of year. The conversation can be about anything at all – the weather, family, the garden – what is important is the connection being made and being generous with your time.

Inviting people around to your own home is another sign that you are happy to make some time to get to know your neighbors, colleagues or anyone else you might have come into contact with through various clubs or hobbies. Offer them a warm greeting as they come in and offer food or drink as soon as they've taken their coat off to create a particularly welcoming environment.

The very essence of hygge is community and social connections – being with people and enjoying their company. It's too easy to put off that get-together, to give in to feeling tired and overwhelmed. Don't worry if the house is not in perfect order or you haven't prepared an eight course feast fit for royalty. Whipping up your favourite, but easy, dish along with a refreshing drink is all that is needed. Embrace the company of others and feed off their vitality and interests, as they will from you. Of course, there are plenty of opportunities for hygge on your own, but when you do get the chance, enjoy the company of others and share your experiences together through a shared meal and conversation.

#27 Avoid controversy

One of the main purposes of hygge is to encourage a sense of community and togetherness in a family or even with someone who might have walked through your front door for the first time ten minutes ago. Its aim is to create an inviting atmosphere, where everyone can feel at ease and comfortable, as if they were sitting in their own home.

Much of this occurs during the preparation for meals and the subsequent eating of them, normally accompanied by drinking and discussion. It's important to understand that the discussions at these occasions are not designed as an opportunity to convince anyone of a political perspective or to win some kind of debate. Try to avoid really controversial issues about which people may feel extremely strongly and be highly emotional. Such conversations can often descend into bitter arguments and subsequent recriminations which will destroy the atmosphere you have worked so hard to create.

If the topic does turn to a particularly controversial topic, then at least allow anyone who wishes, to express their opinion without fear or rebuke or retribution. The dinner table should allow everyone to feel safe in their opinion, not to feel worried that their views are going to be met with hostility. Talk of politics or religion will often lead to arguments which in turn will make promoting positivity very difficult. Avoid feeling the need to "win" an argument or making efforts to bring everyone round to your way of thinking – it's not going to happen and will leave people angry and upset. Encourage conversation at all times, but try and steer the topics away from ones where people will leave the table feeling upset or undervalued.

#28 Involving everyone

Having a conversation that includes everyone, means that all understand that boasting about achievements or your own successes at the expense of others is to be avoided at all costs. Think about how those around will you will receive your news and how it might affect them. Talking about your recent job promotion when others may be struggling at work for, could lead to people feeling upset and worried about their own prospects. Recounting the stories of your latest gadget purchase or your new car, at a time when the focus is on companionship and feeling content with what you currently have, is not going to help the ambience around the dinner table either.

Feel free to talk about yourself, but not at the expense of everyone else. Don't try and hog the limelight by butting in on the stories of other people and twisting the conversation back to you. Listen as much as you talk. When you do talk about yourself, making the story rather self-deprecating, brief or adding humor will help enormously and allow everyone to feel involved.

#29 Focus on the positive

Avoid bringing in negativity or complaints to the table. People who end up moaning about their conditions at work or their co-workers or their salary or how messy their kids are, do little to add to the general well-being of the room. They tend to suck up the positivity and encourage people to feed off them. Before too long, the entire room can end up in a competition to see who is the least well off.

There are certain topics you should make every effort to avoid in discussions to ensure you are always able to keep that air of positivity. Avoid negative topics in general such as world banking collapses or the latest murder in the news. Avoid droning on in detail about something highly technical or a topic that is of limited interest to anyone else.

Being interested in other people, asking questions about them or their experiences and background, and being genuinely interested in what other people have to say will encourage them to open up and talk. Conversation is key to making connections with people. Making the time and space for proper communication, face to face, freed from a keyboard or a telephone will allow you to relate to others and let them know you value their presence and what they say. Good conversation can create a positive environment, where everyone feels comfortable and secure enough to forge strong connections that can last years and years.

Chapter 6 - Hygge at Work

It's great to be able to feel comfortable and warm and happy at home, but if all that is torn away every time you go to work, it can make life very stressful. Dreading going to work will make your time at home full of worry and anxiety, as you are always thinking about the end of the weekend or the holidays and the misery work will bring. It will make feeling good at home impossible, no matter what you do.

It's vital to address this if you are to look at your life as a whole and try to create a happier and more content existence. This chapter looks at how important it is to consider the workplace and your work habits in order to create harmony between work and home.

One of the key features of Danish life and hygge in general is the effort to strike the right balance between work and play. It is far too easy to slip into the habit of answering emails at night or trying to sneak a couple of hours work in to prepare for the next day, at the expense of living in the moment and appreciating what is going on right now.

Part of the reason that Denmark is renowned for its work life balance is the emphasis that society itself places on people being able to get away from work. There is greater flexibility in the work day and there is more vacation time allocated to workers than almost anywhere else in the world. Some of that might be tricky to implement in your personal situation, however there are several easy steps that can be taken to ensure you are able to look at your personal work life balance and check it is still right for you.

Planning ahead

As your commitments to work and family increase over the years, it becomes almost impossible to have a spur of the moment dinner or to ring a friend up with little notice and arrange a meeting. In order to try and get round this, be meticulous in your arrangements and do your utmost to stick to them, no matter what.

Agree to meet your friends on the first Friday of the month for example and make sure it goes ahead as planned. Do the same with your family. Make one particular night a movie night or head off to your local restaurant for a meal. The most important thing is to provide adequate notice and ensure everyone is willing to stick to that time and place.

Build more time in for relaxation

Working harder does not necessarily mean you are being more productive. In fact, it is probably the opposite. Don't feel guilty about taking time out for yourself to relax and unwind. Actively engage with things that you enjoy and reserve that time exclusively.

54

When you return to your task, you will feel more invigorated, ready to work and ultimately better placed to achieve more.

Exercise

This is critical for being able to relax more. Do whatever it is that you enjoy – walking the dog, yoga, taking classes at the gym – all of these will all give you a little time for yourself and enable you to release the stress and tension of the day.

Don't stay at work for no reason

There have been times in my life when I realize I'm at work beyond the time I should be and doing very little. That might be down to habit or perhaps you don't want to be the first person to leave, but always ensure that if you are actually at work, then you are doing something of value.

If you are just sitting there doing very little because you feel obligated to be there late, then simply head home. All bosses appreciate effectiveness and if you can do the job in a shorter time than everyone else to the same standard, then your value is likely to increase rather than decrease.

Take regular breaks

Ensure you are able to build rest into your day. Even if it's just 10 minutes for a quick cup of coffee, that time is critical to ensure you can last the day and continue to work efficiently. Working hours on end without respite will achieve nothing, but leave you exhausted and unable to focus.

Don't take work home

Don't feel you're at work when you're at home. In today's world of devices that are always connected, it is easy to feel trapped and overwhelmed even in your own home as people are always able to reach you. Turn off your 'phone or divert calls. If possible, get another number for work entirely. Don't answer emails when you're at home or you will find people continue to assume you are happy to work. Try and disconnect entirely and give some time to yourself.

Consider flexible time

If it fits, you could ask your employer if having a more flexible work day is possible. You might be surprised how many employers are happy to allow this. It has been shown to increase productivity and makes employees more loyal to a company that is willing to help where it can.

Saying No

This is often very hard for people, but saying no, politely but firmly, is important if you want to maintain that balance. There are only so many things you can do in a day and on occasion there will be times where you simply do not have the time to carry out a task or help out. It's OK to explain that to people and effective communication is critical. You don't have to do every job going and someone else will be able to step in.

Divide the jobs

There are plenty of jobs to do at home and at work. Ensure they are split evenly by allocating tasks to people, so you don't end up doing the lot and feeling that going home is like going to work, but without the pay.

Ask for help

If you feel something is not right at work or at home and you're not coping well, then talk to the important people in your life. That might be a boss at work or your immediate family at home, but once your feelings are known it becomes much easier to formulate a plan to ensure you remain healthy.

Chapter 7 – Contentment

#31 Gratitude

One of the main concepts of hygge is to make an effort to put aside negative emotions such as envy, and to focus on being grateful for where you are and what you have – to be able to feel gratitude.

Being able to express gratitude, even for small things, can be difficult and it is not a skill that comes naturally to many, however it is critical for emotional well-being and mental health.

There are many benefits associated with expressing gratitude. The most obvious of these is that it is an opportunity to understand what we have, rather than continually hankering after things we think we need in order to make ourselves happy. It gives us a chance to look around and appreciate all that we have achieved and where we are in the moment.

Happiness is not going to be reached by buying a new car or television or a pair of shoes. We adapt very quickly when these material targets are reached and before too long our previous ambitions are replaced by new ones.

A newer car, a more spacious house, the latest gadget now become the objects of our affection - if only we could get these we would be happier. Of course, none of that is the key to happiness or contentment.

If we are able to look around and appreciate that there are many things in life about which to feel grateful, we are able to be far more positive in our outlook. Although life can be tough and difficult at times, there are still things for which we can feel grateful. There are good things in life right now, even if we don't have everything we might think we need.

Feeling gratitude encourages us to think about where the things that actually make us happy come from. Feeling gratitude will enable you to feel more optimistic about the present and the future, it will bring more happiness into your life every day and generally leave you with a much stronger positive outlook.

Having a more positive perspective on life brings significant physical benefits. Various studies have shown you are better able to ward off colds and other ailments as your immune system is stronger. You are more ready to get involved in physical exercise which in turn increases your health further.

You care more about yourself and others and are prepared to make the effort to eat well and improve your diet. You know the future is bright and want to be physically healthy to take advantage of the good things coming. It can help you sleep better, it will increase your own well-being and it can help you focus your attention for longer.

In addition to increasing your mental and physical health, expressing gratitude makes you far more socially aware. You can see all the good things that your relationships with friends and family can bring. It makes you more outgoing as you actively seek ways to strengthen relationships.

Other people enjoy being around those with a positive attitude – you feel less lonely and might be a little more forgiving of others. Gratitude solidifies relationships, makes you feel more positive, increases your physical well-being and gives you a chance to focus on what is important – those things which make you happy on a day to day basis.

#32 Be in the moment

Hygge is very much about being in the moment. Put aside the worries of work or the jobs you might have waiting for you at home and try and gain as much contentment and happiness as you can from each particular moment. It doesn't mean you can't think of the future and plan ahead, but it does allow you to relax and recharge yourself to ensure you are better prepared to face whatever lies ahead.

I have described many different ways that this can be achieved with friends and family. Here are a few techniques that you can use for yourself. Practice these when you have a little time. It doesn't have to be for an extended period. Just a few minutes in each day can be spent thinking about yourself and how you can feel more contented for longer. Hygge doesn't have to be just for those colder, winter months. It is a mind-set that can be applied with great success all year around.

Be happy with who you are

Don't be your own worst critic. Don't allow the criticisms of others to get to you. Be a little kinder to yourself. We are hyper-critical of ourselves and are often the first to point out our own faults and over-analyze them. Continually pondering one's own shortcomings is not healthy and ruminating on all the mistakes you think you have made that day will only make matters worse.

Accept that you are human and therefore prone to error. Look to take something positive, no matter how small, from your experiences. Reframe failure as merely a step on the road to success and treat each day as a learning opportunity. Take what you can from the day, put it to one side, and move onto the next.

Give yourself time

Take a short break from whatever you are doing and just be. Don't try to think of anything in particular, but just be aware of whatever thoughts come into your head. Don't try and analyze them or judge them or push them out. Just let them come and then let them go. Be an observer as they flow through your mind.

Notice the way you breathe and the passage of air through your body as you sit. Try a simple breathing exercise: breathe in for 4 seconds, hold it for 7 seconds and then breathe out for 8 seconds. Just sitting in silence will calm you down and leave you feeling greatly refreshed, ready for the rest of the day.

Enjoy what you are doing now

So much of hygge is being in the present. It is far too easy to dismiss what we are doing at the moment and live our life constantly looking forward. We are always seeking to make the future better and to figure out solutions to problems we think lie further down the road.

In doing so, we forget to live in the moment and appreciate what we are doing. Just being in the present and focusing on what you are doing is liberating and will allow you to complete tasks more effectively.

Look around you now and appreciate what you see. Recognise the beauty of the world around you and also the efforts of your friends and family every day. Stop worrying about terrible events in the future that may never happen – it never helped anyone.

Break up your routines

It's all too easy to feel days are merging together when every day is the same. Try and break up the pattern of your day a little, so each day offers something different. You could change the way you go to work for example or your mode of transport.

Sit somewhere different for lunch or go for a walk to a new place. Anything that can change the monotony of routine will be effective at distinguishing one moment from the next and allow you to experience new things.

Take it slowly

Enjoy the meal you are eating. Really savor every moment you spend in a comfy chair reading that eagerly awaited book. Feel the heat of the fire warm your toes as the rain comes down outside. Don't rush to complete whatever it is you are doing in a manic rush to tick off as many items as you can from your to-do list.

Eating, drinking, enjoying company or just sitting quietly alone – whatever it is, try and get as much as you can from the moment. Notice the small things, remove distractions that demand your attention and do not try to do lots of things at once. Take life more slowly.

#33 Contentment

The final way to think of hygge is one of the most important – the idea of bringing contentment into your life. Feeling comfortable in your surroundings, finding the little things in life that bring you joy, connecting meaningfully with people, living in the moment, focusing on what you have rather than what you think you need and concentrating on the positive things in life will all work together and re-inforce each other, making you feel more contented.

The benefits to this are manifold. Your relationships with people around you will strengthen and you will draw strength and vitality from them. You will feel better about yourself and more able to face the cold winter months and beyond.

Your health improves as your positivity rises and you engage more with people and activities. You will be less concerned about owning more and more "stuff" and far more focused on your own happiness and that of others around you.

You will feel better equipped to handle the fast pace of life these days, able to stop for a while just to enjoy what you have and whatever you are doing that day.

Conclusion

We started this book by talking about exactly what is meant by hygge, searching for a particular word or phrase that might best define what this particularly Danish, abstract noun represents. I hope by now, at the end of this book, that you have more of a feeling about exactly what it entails, how you might bring it into your life and why it is so important. It is a word that cannot quite be accurately translated into English, however it is something that you can feel and recognize when it is there.

Hygge is a word that summarizes all of the previous chapters. It is the physical surroundings, your state of mind and your emotional well-being. It might defy an exact one-word translation, however it is something that you can come to feel instinctively within you and share with others. This book has given you many ways which will enable you to bring hygge into your own life at every available opportunity with little effort and a lot of fun at the same time.

I encourage you, no matter where you are or who you are with, whatever the weather, to look for little ways to bring hygge into your days and your nights. It might be as small as lighting a couple of candles and giving yourself five minutes to rest. It might be having a cup of coffee by yourself or sharing a slice of cake with a friend. It might be enjoying the warmth of your home in winter or the feeling of sand beneath your feet as you walk on the beach on a hot summer day.

Whatever you are doing and wherever you are, seek out and cherish these moments and you will find hygge - along with a happier, healthier and ultimately, a more contented life.

Made in the USA
Middletown, DE
10 February 2017